PERSONAL DETAILS

Name	
Address	
Email	
Phone Number	
Fax Number	

LOG BOOK DETAILS

Log Start Date	
Log book Number	

INDEX

PAGE NUMBER	SUBJECT
1	
2	
3	
4	
5	
6	
7	
8	
9	
10	
11	
12	
13	
14	
15	
16	
17	
18	
19	
20	
21	
22	
23	
24	
25	

INDEX

PAGE NUMBER	SUBJECT
26	
27	
28	
29	
30	
31	
32	
33	
34	
35	
36	
37	
38	
39	
40	
41	
42	
43	
44	
45	
46	
47	
48	
49	
50	

INDEX

PAGE NUMBER	SUBJECT
51	
52	
53	
54	
55	
56	
57	
58	
59	
60	
61	
62	
63	
64	
65	
66	
67	
68	
69	
70	
71	
72	
73	
74	
75	

INDEX

PAGE NUMBER	SUBJECT
76	
77	
78	
79	
80	
81	
82	
83	
84	
85	
86	
87	
88	
89	
90	
91	
92	
93	
94	
95	
96	
97	
98	
99	
100	

HUNTING LOG

Date		Start Time		End Time	

Location		Longitude		Latitude	

Terrain	

Co-Hunter(s)	

Weather
(Rain, Hot Windy etc.)

Temperature
Low	High

Barometer

Activity / Sightings

Feeding	☐
Fresh Droppings	☐
Tracks	☐
Traveling	☐
Other	☐

Gear / Set Up

Moon Phase
1st Quarter ☐ ½ Moon ☐ 3rd Quarter ☐ Full Moon ☐

Hunt Details

Time	Species	Size	Location	Weapon	Seen	Shot	Lost	Captured

ADDITIONAL COMMENTS

HUNTING LOG

Date		Start Time		End Time	

Location		Longitude		Latitude	

Terrain

Co-Hunter(s)

Weather	Activity / Sightings		Gear / Set Up
(Rain, Hot Windy etc.)	Feeding	☐	
	Fresh Droppings	☐	
Temperature	Tracks	☐	
Low · High	Traveling	☐	
	Other	☐	
Barometer	**Moon Phase**		
	1st Quarter ☐ ½ Moon ☐ 3rd Quarter ☐ Full Moon ☐		

Hunt Details

Time	Species	Size	Location	Weapon	Seen	Shot	Lost	Captured

ADDITIONAL COMMENTS

HUNTING LOG

Date		Start Time		End Time	

Location		Longitude		Latitude	

Terrain

Co-Hunter(s)

Weather	Activity / Sightings		Gear / Set Up
(Rain, Hot Windy etc.)	Feeding	☐	
	Fresh Droppings	☐	
Temperature	Tracks	☐	
Low High	Traveling	☐	
	Other	☐	
Barometer	**Moon Phase**		
	1st Quarter ☐ ½ Moon ☐ 3rd Quarter ☐ Full Moon ☐		

Hunt Details

Time	Species	Size	Location	Weapon	Seen	Shot	Lost	Captured

ADDITIONAL COMMENTS

HUNTING LOG

Date	Start Time	End Time

Location	Longitude	Latitude

Terrain

Co-Hunter(s)

Weather
(Rain, Hot Windy etc.)

Temperature
Low	High

Barometer

Activity / Sightings
Feeding	☐
Fresh Droppings	☐
Tracks	☐
Traveling	☐
Other	☐

Gear / Set Up

Moon Phase
1st Quarter ☐   ½ Moon ☐   3rd Quarter ☐   Full Moon ☐

Hunt Details

Time	Species	Size	Location	Weapon	Seen	Shot	Lost	Captured

ADDITIONAL COMMENTS

_____
_____
_____
_____
_____

HUNTING LOG

Date		Start Time		End Time	
Location		Longitude		Latitude	
Terrain					
Co-Hunter(s)					

Weather
(Rain, Hot Windy etc.)

Temperature
Low	High

Barometer

Activity / Sightings
Feeding	☐
Fresh Droppings	☐
Tracks	☐
Traveling	☐
Other	☐

Gear / Set Up

Moon Phase
1st Quarter ☐   ½ Moon ☐   3rd Quarter ☐   Full Moon ☐

Hunt Details

Time	Species	Size	Location	Weapon	Seen	Shot	Lost	Captured

ADDITIONAL COMMENTS

HUNTING LOG

Date		Start Time		End Time	

Location | **Longitude** | **Latitude**

Terrain

Co-Hunter(s)

Weather	Activity / Sightings		Gear / Set Up
(Rain, Hot Windy etc.)	Feeding	☐	
	Fresh Droppings	☐	
Temperature	Tracks	☐	
Low	High	Traveling	☐	
	Other	☐	

Barometer | **Moon Phase**

1st Quarter ☐   ½ Moon ☐   3rd Quarter ☐   Full Moon ☐

Hunt Details

Time	Species	Size	Location	Weapon	Seen	Shot	Lost	Captured

ADDITIONAL COMMENTS

HUNTING LOG

Date		Start Time		End Time	
Location			Longitude		Latitude
Terrain					
Co-Hunter(s)					

Weather (Rain, Hot Windy etc.)	Activity / Sightings		Gear / Set Up
	Feeding	☐	
	Fresh Droppings	☐	
Temperature	Tracks	☐	
Low / High	Traveling	☐	
	Other	☐	

Barometer	**Moon Phase**
	1st Quarter ☐ ½ Moon ☐ 3rd Quarter ☐ Full Moon ☐

Hunt Details

Time	Species	Size	Location	Weapon	Seen	Shot	Lost	Captured

ADDITIONAL COMMENTS

_____

_____

_____

_____

_____

HUNTING LOG

Date		Start Time		End Time	
Location		Longitude		Latitude	
Terrain					
Co-Hunter(s)					

Weather	Activity / Sightings		Gear / Set Up
(Rain, Hot Windy etc.)	Feeding ☐		
	Fresh Droppings ☐		
Temperature	Tracks ☐		
Low High	Traveling ☐		
	Other ☐		
Barometer	**Moon Phase**		
	1st Quarter ☐ ½ Moon ☐ 3rd Quarter ☐ Full Moon ☐		

Hunt Details

Time	Species	Size	Location	Weapon	Seen	Shot	Lost	Captured

ADDITIONAL COMMENTS

_____

_____

_____

_____

_____

HUNTING LOG

Date		Start Time		End Time	

Location		Longitude		Latitude	

Terrain

Co-Hunter(s)

Weather	Activity / Sightings		Gear / Set Up
(Rain, Hot Windy etc.)	Feeding	☐	
	Fresh Droppings	☐	
Temperature	Tracks	☐	
Low | High	Traveling	☐	
	Other	☐	
Barometer	**Moon Phase**		
	1st Quarter ☐ ½ Moon ☐ 3rd Quarter ☐ Full Moon ☐		

Hunt Details

Time	Species	Size	Location	Weapon	Seen	Shot	Lost	Captured

ADDITIONAL COMMENTS

HUNTING LOG

Date		Start Time		End Time	

Location		Longitude		Latitude	

Terrain

Co-Hunter(s)

Weather
(Rain, Hot Windy etc.)

Temperature
Low	High

Barometer

Activity / Sightings
Feeding	☐
Fresh Droppings	☐
Tracks	☐
Traveling	☐
Other	☐

Gear / Set Up

Moon Phase
1st Quarter ☐   ½ Moon ☐   3rd Quarter ☐   Full Moon ☐

Hunt Details

Time	Species	Size	Location	Weapon	Seen	Shot	Lost	Captured

ADDITIONAL COMMENTS

_____
_____
_____
_____
_____

HUNTING LOG

11

| Date | | Start Time | | End Time | |

Location **Longitude** **Latitude**

Terrain

Co-Hunter(s)

Weather	Activity / Sightings		Gear / Set Up
(Rain, Hot Windy etc.)	Feeding	☐	
	Fresh Droppings	☐	
Temperature	Tracks	☐	
Low · High	Traveling	☐	
	Other	☐	
Barometer	**Moon Phase**		

1st Quarter ☐   ½ Moon ☐   3rd Quarter ☐   Full Moon ☐

Hunt Details

Time	Species	Size	Location	Weapon	Seen	Shot	Lost	Captured

ADDITIONAL COMMENTS

HUNTING LOG

Date		Start Time		End Time	

Location		Longitude		Latitude	

Terrain

Co-Hunter(s)

Weather (Rain, Hot Windy etc.)	Activity / Sightings		Gear / Set Up
	Feeding	☐	
	Fresh Droppings	☐	
Temperature	Tracks	☐	
Low | High	Traveling	☐	
	Other	☐	

Barometer

Moon Phase

1st Quarter ☐   ½ Moon ☐   3rd Quarter ☐   Full Moon ☐

Hunt Details

Time	Species	Size	Location	Weapon	Seen	Shot	Lost	Captured

ADDITIONAL COMMENTS

_____
_____
_____
_____
_____

HUNTING LOG

Date		Start Time		End Time	

Location		Longitude		Latitude	

Terrain	

Co-Hunter(s)	

Weather (Rain, Hot Windy etc.)	Activity / Sightings		Gear / Set Up
	Feeding ☐		
	Fresh Droppings ☐		
Temperature	Tracks ☐		
Low | High	Traveling ☐		
	Other ☐		
Barometer	**Moon Phase**		
	1st Quarter ☐ ½ Moon ☐ 3rd Quarter ☐ Full Moon ☐		

Hunt Details

Time	Species	Size	Location	Weapon	Seen	Shot	Lost	Captured

ADDITIONAL COMMENTS

HUNTING LOG

Date	**Start Time**	**End Time**
Location	**Longitude**	**Latitude**
Terrain		
Co-Hunter(s)		

Weather	Activity / Sightings	Gear / Set Up
(Rain, Hot Windy etc.)	Feeding ☐	
	Fresh Droppings ☐	
Temperature	Tracks ☐	
Low / High	Traveling ☐	
	Other ☐	
Barometer	**Moon Phase**	
	1st Quarter ☐ ½ Moon ☐ 3rd Quarter ☐ Full Moon ☐	

Hunt Details

Time	Species	Size	Location	Weapon	Seen	Shot	Lost	Captured

ADDITIONAL COMMENTS

HUNTING LOG

Date		Start Time		End Time	
Location			Longitude		Latitude
Terrain					
Co-Hunter(s)					

Weather	Activity / Sightings		Gear / Set Up
(Rain, Hot Windy etc.)	Feeding	☐	
	Fresh Droppings	☐	
Temperature	Tracks	☐	
Low High	Traveling	☐	
	Other	☐	
Barometer	**Moon Phase**		
	1st Quarter ☐ ½ Moon ☐ 3rd Quarter ☐ Full Moon ☐		

Hunt Details

Time	Species	Size	Location	Weapon	Seen	Shot	Lost	Captured

ADDITIONAL COMMENTS

HUNTING LOG

Date		Start Time		End Time	

Location		Longitude		Latitude	

Terrain

Co-Hunter(s)

Weather (Rain, Hot Windy etc.)	**Activity / Sightings**		**Gear / Set Up**
	Feeding	☐	
	Fresh Droppings	☐	
Temperature	Tracks	☐	
Low High	Traveling	☐	
	Other	☐	
Barometer	**Moon Phase**		
	1st Quarter ☐ ½ Moon ☐ 3rd Quarter ☐ Full Moon ☐		

Hunt Details

Time	Species	Size	Location	Weapon	Seen	Shot	Lost	Captured

ADDITIONAL COMMENTS

_____

_____

_____

_____

_____

HUNTING LOG

Date		Start Time		End Time	

Location		Longitude		Latitude	

Terrain

Co-Hunter(s)

Weather	Activity / Sightings		Gear / Set Up
(Rain, Hot Windy etc.)	Feeding	☐	
	Fresh Droppings	☐	
Temperature	Tracks	☐	
Low High	Traveling	☐	
	Other	☐	

Barometer   **Moon Phase**

1st Quarter ☐   ½ Moon ☐   3rd Quarter ☐   Full Moon ☐

Hunt Details

Time	Species	Size	Location	Weapon	Seen	Shot	Lost	Captured

ADDITIONAL COMMENTS

_____

_____

_____

_____

_____

HUNTING LOG

Date		Start Time		End Time	

Location | **Longitude** | **Latitude**

Terrain

Co-Hunter(s)

Weather (Rain, Hot Windy etc.)	**Activity / Sightings**		**Gear / Set Up**
	Feeding	☐	
	Fresh Droppings	☐	
Temperature	Tracks	☐	
Low High	Traveling	☐	
	Other	☐	
Barometer	**Moon Phase**		
	1st Quarter ☐ ½ Moon ☐ 3rd Quarter ☐ Full Moon ☐		

Hunt Details

Time	Species	Size	Location	Weapon	Seen	Shot	Lost	Captured

ADDITIONAL COMMENTS

_____

_____

_____

_____

_____

HUNTING LOG

Date		Start Time		End Time	

Location		Longitude		Latitude	

Terrain

Co-Hunter(s)

Weather	Activity / Sightings	Gear / Set Up
(Rain, Hot Windy etc.)		

Weather (Rain, Hot Windy etc.)

Activity / Sightings

Feeding	☐
Fresh Droppings	☐
Tracks	☐
Traveling	☐
Other	☐

Temperature

Low	High

Gear / Set Up

Barometer

Moon Phase

1st Quarter ☐ ½ Moon ☐ 3rd Quarter ☐ Full Moon ☐

Hunt Details

Time	Species	Size	Location	Weapon	Seen	Shot	Lost	Captured

ADDITIONAL COMMENTS

_____

_____

_____

_____

_____

HUNTING LOG

| Date | | Start Time | | End Time | |

| Location | | Longitude | | Latitude | |

| Terrain | |

| Co-Hunter(s) | |

Weather
(Rain, Hot Windy etc.)

Temperature
| Low | High |

Barometer

Activity / Sightings
Feeding	☐
Fresh Droppings	☐
Tracks	☐
Traveling	☐
Other	☐

Gear / Set Up

Moon Phase
1st Quarter ☐   ½ Moon ☐   3rd Quarter ☐   Full Moon ☐

Hunt Details

Time	Species	Size	Location	Weapon	Seen	Shot	Lost	Captured

ADDITIONAL COMMENTS

HUNTING LOG

Date	Start Time	End Time

Location	Longitude	Latitude

Terrain

Co-Hunter(s)

Weather	Activity / Sightings		Gear / Set Up
(Rain, Hot Windy etc.)	Feeding	☐	
	Fresh Droppings	☐	
Temperature	Tracks	☐	
Low High	Traveling	☐	
	Other	☐	
Barometer	**Moon Phase**		
	1st Quarter ☐ ½ Moon ☐ 3rd Quarter ☐ Full Moon ☐		

Hunt Details

Time	Species	Size	Location	Weapon	Seen	Shot	Lost	Captured

ADDITIONAL COMMENTS

HUNTING LOG

Date		Start Time		End Time	

Location		Longitude		Latitude	

Terrain

Co-Hunter(s)

Weather	Activity / Sightings		Gear / Set Up
(Rain, Hot Windy etc.)	Feeding	☐	
	Fresh Droppings	☐	
Temperature	Tracks	☐	
Low High	Traveling	☐	
	Other	☐	
Barometer	**Moon Phase**		
	1st Quarter ☐ ½ Moon ☐ 3rd Quarter ☐ Full Moon ☐		

Hunt Details

Time	Species	Size	Location	Weapon	Seen	Shot	Lost	Captured

ADDITIONAL COMMENTS

_____

_____

_____

_____

_____

HUNTING LOG

Date		Start Time		End Time	

Location		Longitude		Latitude	

Terrain

Co-Hunter(s)

Weather	Activity / Sightings		Gear / Set Up
(Rain, Hot Windy etc.)	Feeding	☐	
	Fresh Droppings	☐	
Temperature	Tracks	☐	
Low | High	Traveling	☐	
	Other	☐	
Barometer	**Moon Phase**		

1st Quarter ☐   ½ Moon ☐   3rd Quarter ☐   Full Moon ☐

Hunt Details

Time	Species	Size	Location	Weapon	Seen	Shot	Lost	Captured

ADDITIONAL COMMENTS

_____
_____
_____
_____
_____

HUNTING LOG

Date		Start Time		End Time	

Location		Longitude		Latitude	

Terrain

Co-Hunter(s)

Weather	Activity / Sightings		Gear / Set Up
(Rain, Hot Windy etc.)	Feeding	☐	
	Fresh Droppings	☐	
Temperature	Tracks	☐	
Low / High	Traveling	☐	
	Other	☐	

Barometer	**Moon Phase**
	1st Quarter ☐ ½ Moon ☐ 3rd Quarter ☐ Full Moon ☐

Hunt Details

Time	Species	Size	Location	Weapon	Seen	Shot	Lost	Captured

ADDITIONAL COMMENTS

_____

_____

_____

_____

_____

HUNTING LOG

Date		Start Time		End Time	

Location		Longitude		Latitude	

Terrain

Co-Hunter(s)

Weather	Activity / Sightings		Gear / Set Up
(Rain, Hot Windy etc.)	Feeding	☐	
	Fresh Droppings	☐	
Temperature	Tracks	☐	
Low High	Traveling	☐	
	Other	☐	
Barometer	**Moon Phase**		
	1st Quarter ☐ ½ Moon ☐ 3rd Quarter ☐ Full Moon ☐		

Hunt Details

Time	Species	Size	Location	Weapon	Seen	Shot	Lost	Captured

ADDITIONAL COMMENTS

HUNTING LOG

26

Date		Start Time		End Time	

Location		Longitude		Latitude	

Terrain	

Co-Hunter(s)	

Weather	Activity / Sightings		Gear / Set Up
(Rain, Hot Windy etc.)	Feeding	☐	
	Fresh Droppings	☐	
Temperature	Tracks	☐	
Low High	Traveling	☐	
	Other	☐	
Barometer	**Moon Phase**		
	1st Quarter ☐ ½ Moon ☐ 3rd Quarter ☐ Full Moon ☐		

Hunt Details

Time	Species	Size	Location	Weapon	Seen	Shot	Lost	Captured

ADDITIONAL COMMENTS

_____
_____
_____
_____
_____

HUNTING LOG

27

Date	Start Time	End Time

Location	Longitude	Latitude

Terrain

Co-Hunter(s)

Weather	Activity / Sightings		Gear / Set Up
(Rain, Hot Windy etc.)	Feeding	☐	
	Fresh Droppings	☐	
Temperature	Tracks	☐	
Low High	Traveling	☐	
	Other	☐	
Barometer	**Moon Phase**		
	1st Quarter ☐ ½ Moon ☐ 3rd Quarter ☐ Full Moon ☐		

Hunt Details

Time	Species	Size	Location	Weapon	Seen	Shot	Lost	Captured

ADDITIONAL COMMENTS

HUNTING LOG

Date	Start Time	End Time

Location	Longitude	Latitude

Terrain

Co-Hunter(s)

Weather (Rain, Hot Windy etc.)	**Activity / Sightings**	**Gear / Set Up**

Activity / Sightings

Feeding	☐
Fresh Droppings	☐
Tracks	☐
Traveling	☐
Other	☐

Temperature

Low	High

Barometer

Moon Phase

1st Quarter ☐   ½ Moon ☐   3rd Quarter ☐   Full Moon ☐

Hunt Details

Time	Species	Size	Location	Weapon	Seen	Shot	Lost	Captured

ADDITIONAL COMMENTS

HUNTING LOG

Date		Start Time		End Time	

Location		Longitude		Latitude	

Terrain

Co-Hunter(s)

Weather	Activity / Sightings		Gear / Set Up
(Rain, Hot Windy etc.)	Feeding	☐	
	Fresh Droppings	☐	
Temperature	Tracks	☐	
Low | High	Traveling	☐	
	Other	☐	

Barometer

Moon Phase

1st Quarter ☐   ½ Moon ☐   3rd Quarter ☐   Full Moon ☐

Hunt Details

Time	Species	Size	Location	Weapon	Seen	Shot	Lost	Captured

ADDITIONAL COMMENTS

_____

_____

_____

_____

_____

HUNTING LOG

Date		Start Time		End Time	

Location		Longitude		Latitude	

Terrain	

Co-Hunter(s)	

Weather (Rain, Hot Windy etc.)	Activity / Sightings		Gear / Set Up
	Feeding	☐	
	Fresh Droppings	☐	
Temperature	Tracks	☐	
Low · High	Traveling	☐	
	Other	☐	
Barometer	**Moon Phase**		

1st Quarter ☐   ½ Moon ☐   3rd Quarter ☐   Full Moon ☐

Hunt Details

Time	Species	Size	Location	Weapon	Seen	Shot	Lost	Captured

ADDITIONAL COMMENTS

_____

_____

_____

_____

_____

HUNTING LOG

Date		Start Time		End Time	

Location		Longitude		Latitude	

Terrain

Co-Hunter(s)

Weather	Activity / Sightings		Gear / Set Up
(Rain, Hot Windy etc.)	Feeding	☐	
	Fresh Droppings	☐	
Temperature	Tracks	☐	
Low / High	Traveling	☐	
	Other	☐	
Barometer	**Moon Phase**		
	1st Quarter ☐ ½ Moon ☐ 3rd Quarter ☐ Full Moon ☐		

Hunt Details

Time	Species	Size	Location	Weapon	Seen	Shot	Lost	Captured

ADDITIONAL COMMENTS

_____

_____

_____

_____

_____

HUNTING LOG

Date		Start Time		End Time	

Location		Longitude		Latitude	

Terrain	

Co-Hunter(s)	

Weather	Activity / Sightings		Gear / Set Up
(Rain, Hot Windy etc.)	Feeding	☐	
	Fresh Droppings	☐	
Temperature	Tracks	☐	
Low High	Traveling	☐	
	Other	☐	
Barometer	**Moon Phase**		
	1st Quarter ☐ ½ Moon ☐ 3rd Quarter ☐ Full Moon ☐		

Hunt Details

Time	Species	Size	Location	Weapon	Seen	Shot	Lost	Captured

ADDITIONAL COMMENTS

Date		Start Time		End Time	

Location		Longitude		Latitude	

Terrain	

Co-Hunter(s)	

Weather	Activity / Sightings		Gear / Set Up
(Rain, Hot Windy etc.)	Feeding	☐	
	Fresh Droppings	☐	
Temperature	Tracks	☐	
Low | High	Traveling	☐	
	Other	☐	
Barometer	**Moon Phase**		
	1st Quarter ☐ ½ Moon ☐ 3rd Quarter ☐ Full Moon ☐		

Hunt Details

Time	Species	Size	Location	Weapon	Seen	Shot	Lost	Captured

ADDITIONAL COMMENTS

HUNTING LOG

Date		Start Time		End Time	

Location		Longitude		Latitude	

Terrain

Co-Hunter(s)

Weather	Activity / Sightings	Gear / Set Up
(Rain, Hot Windy etc.)	Feeding ☐	
	Fresh Droppings ☐	
Temperature	Tracks ☐	
Low | High	Traveling ☐	
	Other ☐	
Barometer	**Moon Phase**	
	1st Quarter ☐ ½ Moon ☐ 3rd Quarter ☐ Full Moon ☐	

Hunt Details

Time	Species	Size	Location	Weapon	Seen	Shot	Lost	Captured

ADDITIONAL COMMENTS

_____
_____
_____
_____
_____

HUNTING LOG

Date	Start Time	End Time

Location	Longitude	Latitude

Terrain

Co-Hunter(s)

Weather (Rain, Hot Windy etc.)	**Activity / Sightings**		**Gear / Set Up**
	Feeding	☐	
	Fresh Droppings	☐	
Temperature	Tracks	☐	
Low	High	Traveling	☐
	Other	☐	
Barometer	**Moon Phase**		

1st Quarter ☐   ½ Moon ☐   3rd Quarter ☐   Full Moon ☐

Hunt Details

Time	Species	Size	Location	Weapon	Seen	Shot	Lost	Captured

ADDITIONAL COMMENTS

HUNTING LOG

Date		Start Time		End Time	

Location		Longitude		Latitude	

Terrain

Co-Hunter(s)

Weather		Activity / Sightings		Gear / Set Up
(Rain, Hot Windy etc.)		Feeding ☐		
		Fresh Droppings ☐		
Temperature		Tracks ☐		
Low	High	Traveling ☐		
		Other ☐		
Barometer		**Moon Phase**		

1st Quarter ☐   ½ Moon ☐   3rd Quarter ☐   Full Moon ☐

Hunt Details

Time	Species	Size	Location	Weapon	Seen	Shot	Lost	Captured

ADDITIONAL COMMENTS

_____
_____
_____
_____
_____

HUNTING LOG

Date		Start Time		End Time	

Location | **Longitude** | **Latitude**

Terrain

Co-Hunter(s)

Weather	Activity / Sightings		Gear / Set Up
(Rain, Hot Windy etc.)	Feeding	☐	
	Fresh Droppings	☐	
Temperature	Tracks	☐	
Low High	Traveling	☐	
	Other	☐	
Barometer	**Moon Phase**		

1st Quarter ☐   ½ Moon ☐   3rd Quarter ☐   Full Moon ☐

Hunt Details

Time	Species	Size	Location	Weapon	Seen	Shot	Lost	Captured

ADDITIONAL COMMENTS

HUNTING LOG

Date **Start Time** **End Time**

Location **Longitude** **Latitude**

Terrain

Co-Hunter(s)

Weather (Rain, Hot Windy etc.)	Activity / Sightings		Gear / Set Up
	Feeding	☐	
	Fresh Droppings	☐	
Temperature	Tracks	☐	
Low — High	Traveling	☐	
	Other	☐	

Barometer	**Moon Phase**
	1st Quarter ☐ ½ Moon ☐ 3rd Quarter ☐ Full Moon ☐

Hunt Details

Time	Species	Size	Location	Weapon	Seen	Shot	Lost	Captured

ADDITIONAL COMMENTS

_____
_____
_____
_____
_____

HUNTING LOG

Date		Start Time		End Time	

Location		Longitude		Latitude	

Terrain

Co-Hunter(s)

Weather	Activity / Sightings		Gear / Set Up
(Rain, Hot Windy etc.)	Feeding	☐	
	Fresh Droppings	☐	
Temperature	Tracks	☐	
Low ǀ High	Traveling	☐	
	Other	☐	
Barometer	**Moon Phase**		
	1st Quarter ☐ ½ Moon ☐ 3rd Quarter ☐ Full Moon ☐		

Hunt Details

Time	Species	Size	Location	Weapon	Seen	Shot	Lost	Captured

ADDITIONAL COMMENTS

HUNTING LOG

40

| Date | | Start Time | | End Time | |

Date | **Start Time** | **End Time**

Location | **Longitude** | **Latitude**

Terrain

Co-Hunter(s)

Weather (Rain, Hot Windy etc.)	**Activity / Sightings**	**Gear / Set Up**
	Feeding ☐	
	Fresh Droppings ☐	
Temperature	Tracks ☐	
Low | High	Traveling ☐	
	Other ☐	

Barometer	**Moon Phase**
	1st Quarter ☐ ½ Moon ☐ 3rd Quarter ☐ Full Moon ☐

Hunt Details

Time	Species	Size	Location	Weapon	Seen	Shot	Lost	Captured

ADDITIONAL COMMENTS

HUNTING LOG

Date		Start Time		End Time	

Location		Longitude		Latitude	

Terrain

Co-Hunter(s)

Weather	Activity / Sightings		Gear / Set Up
(Rain, Hot Windy etc.)	Feeding	☐	
	Fresh Droppings	☐	
Temperature	Tracks	☐	
Low High	Traveling	☐	
	Other	☐	
Barometer	**Moon Phase**		
	1st Quarter ☐ ½ Moon ☐ 3rd Quarter ☐ Full Moon ☐		

Hunt Details

Time	Species	Size	Location	Weapon	Seen	Shot	Lost	Captured

ADDITIONAL COMMENTS

HUNTING LOG

Date		Start Time		End Time	

Location		Longitude		Latitude	

Terrain

Co-Hunter(s)

Weather	Activity / Sightings		Gear / Set Up
(Rain, Hot Windy etc.)	Feeding	☐	
	Fresh Droppings	☐	
Temperature	Tracks	☐	
Low ǀ High	Traveling	☐	
	Other	☐	

Barometer	**Moon Phase**
	1st Quarter ☐ ½ Moon ☐ 3rd Quarter ☐ Full Moon ☐

Hunt Details

Time	Species	Size	Location	Weapon	Seen	Shot	Lost	Captured

ADDITIONAL COMMENTS

HUNTING LOG

Date		Start Time		End Time	

Location   **Longitude**   **Latitude**

Terrain

Co-Hunter(s)

Weather (Rain, Hot Windy etc.)	Activity / Sightings		Gear / Set Up
	Feeding	☐	
	Fresh Droppings	☐	
Temperature	Tracks	☐	
Low High	Traveling	☐	
	Other	☐	
Barometer	**Moon Phase**		

1st Quarter ☐   ½ Moon ☐   3rd Quarter ☐   Full Moon ☐

Hunt Details

Time	Species	Size	Location	Weapon	Seen	Shot	Lost	Captured

ADDITIONAL COMMENTS

_____
_____
_____
_____
_____

HUNTING LOG

Date		Start Time		End Time	

Location		Longitude		Latitude	

Terrain	

Co-Hunter(s)	

Weather (Rain, Hot Windy etc.)	Activity / Sightings	Gear / Set Up

Activity / Sightings
- Feeding ☐
- Fresh Droppings ☐
- Tracks ☐
- Traveling ☐
- Other ☐

Temperature
Low	High

Barometer

Moon Phase
1st Quarter ☐ ½ Moon ☐ 3rd Quarter ☐ Full Moon ☐

Hunt Details

Time	Species	Size	Location	Weapon	Seen	Shot	Lost	Captured

ADDITIONAL COMMENTS

_____
_____
_____
_____
_____

Date	Start Time	End Time

Location	Longitude	Latitude

Terrain

Co-Hunter(s)

Weather (Rain, Hot Windy etc.)	Activity / Sightings		Gear / Set Up
	Feeding	☐	
	Fresh Droppings	☐	
Temperature	Tracks	☐	
Low | High	Traveling	☐	
	Other	☐	
Barometer	**Moon Phase**		
	1st Quarter ☐ ½ Moon ☐ 3rd Quarter ☐ Full Moon ☐		

Hunt Details

Time	Species	Size	Location	Weapon	Seen	Shot	Lost	Captured

ADDITIONAL COMMENTS

_____

_____

_____

_____

_____

HUNTING LOG

46

Date		Start Time		End Time	

Location		Longitude		Latitude	

Terrain

Co-Hunter(s)

Weather	Activity / Sightings		Gear / Set Up
(Rain, Hot Windy etc.)	Feeding	☐	
	Fresh Droppings	☐	
Temperature	Tracks	☐	
Low High	Traveling	☐	
	Other	☐	
Barometer	**Moon Phase**		
	1st Quarter ☐ ½ Moon ☐ 3rd Quarter ☐ Full Moon ☐		

Hunt Details

Time	Species	Size	Location	Weapon	Seen	Shot	Lost	Captured

ADDITIONAL COMMENTS

HUNTING LOG

Date		Start Time		End Time	

Location		Longitude		Latitude	

Terrain

Co-Hunter(s)

Weather (Rain, Hot Windy etc.)	Activity / Sightings		Gear / Set Up
	Feeding	☐	
	Fresh Droppings	☐	
Temperature	Tracks	☐	
Low | High	Traveling	☐	
	Other	☐	
Barometer	**Moon Phase**		
	1st Quarter ☐ ½ Moon ☐ 3rd Quarter ☐ Full Moon ☐		

Hunt Details

Time	Species	Size	Location	Weapon	Seen	Shot	Lost	Captured

ADDITIONAL COMMENTS

HUNTING LOG

Date		Start Time		End Time	
Location		Longitude		Latitude	
Terrain					
Co-Hunter(s)					

Weather
(Rain, Hot Windy etc.)

Temperature
Low	High

Barometer

Activity / Sightings
Feeding	☐
Fresh Droppings	☐
Tracks	☐
Traveling	☐
Other	☐

Gear / Set Up

Moon Phase
1st Quarter ☐ ½ Moon ☐ 3rd Quarter ☐ Full Moon ☐

Hunt Details

Time	Species	Size	Location	Weapon	Seen	Shot	Lost	Captured

ADDITIONAL COMMENTS

_____
_____
_____
_____

HUNTING LOG

49

Date		Start Time		End Time	

Location		Longitude		Latitude	

Terrain	

Co-Hunter(s)	

Weather (Rain, Hot Windy etc.)	Activity / Sightings	Gear / Set Up

Activity / Sightings	
Feeding	☐
Fresh Droppings	☐
Tracks	☐
Traveling	☐
Other	☐

Temperature
Low | High

Barometer

Moon Phase

1st Quarter ☐   ½ Moon ☐   3rd Quarter ☐   Full Moon ☐

Hunt Details

Time	Species	Size	Location	Weapon	Seen	Shot	Lost	Captured

ADDITIONAL COMMENTS

HUNTING LOG

Date	Start Time	End Time
Location	Longitude	Latitude
Terrain		
Co-Hunter(s)		

Weather	Activity / Sightings	Gear / Set Up
(Rain, Hot Windy etc.)	Feeding ☐	
	Fresh Droppings ☐	
Temperature	Tracks ☐	
Low / High	Traveling ☐	
	Other ☐	

Barometer	Moon Phase
	1st Quarter ☐ ½ Moon ☐ 3rd Quarter ☐ Full Moon ☐

Hunt Details

Time	Species	Size	Location	Weapon	Seen	Shot	Lost	Captured

ADDITIONAL COMMENTS

_____
_____
_____
_____
_____

HUNTING LOG

Date		Start Time		End Time	

Location		Longitude		Latitude	

Terrain

Co-Hunter(s)

Weather	Activity / Sightings		Gear / Set Up
(Rain, Hot Windy etc.)	Feeding	☐	
	Fresh Droppings	☐	
Temperature	Tracks	☐	
Low High	Traveling	☐	
	Other	☐	
Barometer	**Moon Phase**		
	1st Quarter ☐ ½ Moon ☐ 3rd Quarter ☐ Full Moon ☐		

Hunt Details

Time	Species	Size	Location	Weapon	Seen	Shot	Lost	Captured

ADDITIONAL COMMENTS

_____

_____

_____

_____

_____

HUNTING LOG

| Date | | Start Time | | End Time | |

| Location | | Longitude | | Latitude | |

| Terrain | |

| Co-Hunter(s) | |

Weather	**Activity / Sightings**		**Gear / Set Up**
(Rain, Hot Windy etc.)	Feeding	☐	
	Fresh Droppings	☐	
Temperature	Tracks	☐	
Low | High	Traveling	☐	
	Other	☐	

Barometer	**Moon Phase**
	1st Quarter ☐ ½ Moon ☐ 3rd Quarter ☐ Full Moon ☐

Hunt Details

Time	Species	Size	Location	Weapon	Seen	Shot	Lost	Captured

ADDITIONAL COMMENTS

_____

_____

_____

_____

_____

HUNTING LOG

Date		Start Time		End Time	

Location | **Longitude** | **Latitude**

Terrain

Co-Hunter(s)

Weather	Activity / Sightings		Gear / Set Up
(Rain, Hot Windy etc.)	Feeding	☐	
	Fresh Droppings	☐	
Temperature	Tracks	☐	
Low High	Traveling	☐	
	Other	☐	

Barometer   **Moon Phase**

1st Quarter ☐   ½ Moon ☐   3rd Quarter ☐   Full Moon ☐

Hunt Details

Time	Species	Size	Location	Weapon	Seen	Shot	Lost	Captured

ADDITIONAL COMMENTS

HUNTING LOG

Date		Start Time		End Time	

Location		Longitude		Latitude	

Terrain

Co-Hunter(s)

Weather (Rain, Hot Windy etc.)	**Activity / Sightings**		**Gear / Set Up**
	Feeding	☐	
	Fresh Droppings	☐	
Temperature	Tracks	☐	
Low | High	Traveling	☐	
	Other	☐	
Barometer	**Moon Phase**		
	1st Quarter ☐ ½ Moon ☐ 3rd Quarter ☐ Full Moon ☐		

Hunt Details

Time	Species	Size	Location	Weapon	Seen	Shot	Lost	Captured

ADDITIONAL COMMENTS

HUNTING LOG

Date		Start Time		End Time	

Location		Longitude		Latitude	

Terrain

Co-Hunter(s)

Weather	Activity / Sightings	Gear / Set Up
(Rain, Hot Windy etc.)	Feeding ☐	
	Fresh Droppings ☐	
Temperature	Tracks ☐	
Low | High	Traveling ☐	
	Other ☐	

Barometer	Moon Phase
	1st Quarter ☐ ½ Moon ☐ 3rd Quarter ☐ Full Moon ☐

Hunt Details

Time	Species	Size	Location	Weapon	Seen	Shot	Lost	Captured

ADDITIONAL COMMENTS

_____

_____

_____

_____

_____

HUNTING LOG

Date | **Start Time** | **End Time**

Location | **Longitude** | **Latitude**

Terrain

Co-Hunter(s)

Weather (Rain, Hot Windy etc.)	Activity / Sightings		Gear / Set Up
	Feeding	☐	
	Fresh Droppings	☐	
Temperature	Tracks	☐	
Low | High	Traveling	☐	
	Other	☐	
Barometer	**Moon Phase**		
	1st Quarter ☐ ½ Moon ☐ 3rd Quarter ☐ Full Moon ☐		

Hunt Details

Time	Species	Size	Location	Weapon	Seen	Shot	Lost	Captured

ADDITIONAL COMMENTS

HUNTING LOG

Date

Start Time

End Time

Location

Longitude

Latitude

Terrain

Co-Hunter(s)

Weather (Rain, Hot Windy etc.)	Activity / Sightings		Gear / Set Up
	Feeding	☐	
	Fresh Droppings	☐	
Temperature	Tracks	☐	
Low High	Traveling	☐	
	Other	☐	
Barometer	**Moon Phase**		
	1st Quarter ☐ ½ Moon ☐ 3rd Quarter ☐ Full Moon ☐		

Hunt Details

Time	Species	Size	Location	Weapon	Seen	Shot	Lost	Captured

ADDITIONAL COMMENTS

HUNTING LOG

58

Date		Start Time		End Time	

Location		Longitude		Latitude	

Terrain

Co-Hunter(s)

Weather (Rain, Hot Windy etc.)	**Activity / Sightings**		**Gear / Set Up**
	Feeding	☐	
	Fresh Droppings	☐	
Temperature	Tracks	☐	
Low / High	Traveling	☐	
	Other	☐	

Barometer	**Moon Phase**
	1st Quarter ☐ ½ Moon ☐ 3rd Quarter ☐ Full Moon ☐

Hunt Details

Time	Species	Size	Location	Weapon	Seen	Shot	Lost	Captured

ADDITIONAL COMMENTS

_____
_____
_____
_____
_____

HUNTING LOG

Date		Start Time		End Time	
Location			Longitude		Latitude
Terrain					
Co-Hunter(s)					

Weather	Activity / Sightings		Gear / Set Up
(Rain, Hot Windy etc.)	Feeding	☐	
	Fresh Droppings	☐	
Temperature	Tracks	☐	
Low / High	Traveling	☐	
	Other	☐	

Barometer

Moon Phase

1st Quarter ☐   ½ Moon ☐   3rd Quarter ☐   Full Moon ☐

Hunt Details

Time	Species	Size	Location	Weapon	Seen	Shot	Lost	Captured

ADDITIONAL COMMENTS

_____

_____

_____

_____

_____

HUNTING LOG

Date		Start Time		End Time	

Location		Longitude		Latitude	

Terrain

Co-Hunter(s)

Weather	Activity / Sightings		Gear / Set Up
(Rain, Hot Windy etc.)	Feeding	☐	
	Fresh Droppings	☐	
Temperature	Tracks	☐	
Low / High	Traveling	☐	
	Other	☐	
Barometer	**Moon Phase**		
	1st Quarter ☐ ½ Moon ☐ 3rd Quarter ☐ Full Moon ☐		

Hunt Details

Time	Species	Size	Location	Weapon	Seen	Shot	Lost	Captured

ADDITIONAL COMMENTS

HUNTING LOG

Date		Start Time		End Time	

Location		Longitude		Latitude	

Terrain

Co-Hunter(s)

Weather	Activity / Sightings		Gear / Set Up
(Rain, Hot Windy etc.)	Feeding	☐	
	Fresh Droppings	☐	
Temperature	Tracks	☐	
Low | High	Traveling	☐	
	Other	☐	

Barometer

Moon Phase

1st Quarter ☐   ½ Moon ☐   3rd Quarter ☐   Full Moon ☐

Hunt Details

Time	Species	Size	Location	Weapon	Seen	Shot	Lost	Captured

ADDITIONAL COMMENTS

_____

_____

_____

_____

_____

HUNTING LOG

Date		Start Time		End Time	

Location		Longitude		Latitude	

Terrain

Co-Hunter(s)

Weather	Activity / Sightings		Gear / Set Up
(Rain, Hot Windy etc.)	Feeding	☐	
	Fresh Droppings	☐	
Temperature	Tracks	☐	
Low	High	Traveling	☐	
	Other	☐	

Barometer	Moon Phase
	1st Quarter ☐ ½ Moon ☐ 3rd Quarter ☐ Full Moon ☐

Hunt Details

Time	Species	Size	Location	Weapon	Seen	Shot	Lost	Captured

ADDITIONAL COMMENTS

Date		Start Time		End Time	

Location		Longitude		Latitude	

Terrain	

Co-Hunter(s)	

Weather (Rain, Hot Windy etc.)	**Activity / Sightings**		**Gear / Set Up**
	Feeding	☐	
	Fresh Droppings	☐	
Temperature	Tracks	☐	
Low High	Traveling	☐	
	Other	☐	
Barometer	**Moon Phase**		
	1st Quarter ☐ ½ Moon ☐ 3rd Quarter ☐ Full Moon ☐		

Hunt Details

Time	Species	Size	Location	Weapon	Seen	Shot	Lost	Captured

ADDITIONAL COMMENTS

_____

_____

_____

_____

_____

HUNTING LOG

Date		Start Time		End Time	
Location		Longitude		Latitude	
Terrain					
Co-Hunter(s)					

Weather	Activity / Sightings		Gear / Set Up
(Rain, Hot Windy etc.)	Feeding	☐	
	Fresh Droppings	☐	
Temperature	Tracks	☐	
Low | High	Traveling	☐	
	Other	☐	
Barometer	**Moon Phase**		
	1st Quarter ☐ ½ Moon ☐ 3rd Quarter ☐ Full Moon ☐		

Hunt Details

Time	Species	Size	Location	Weapon	Seen	Shot	Lost	Captured

ADDITIONAL COMMENTS

_____

_____

_____

_____

_____

Date		Start Time		End Time	
Location		Longitude		Latitude	
Terrain					
Co-Hunter(s)					

Weather	Activity / Sightings		Gear / Set Up
(Rain, Hot Windy etc.)	Feeding	☐	
	Fresh Droppings	☐	
Temperature	Tracks	☐	
Low / High	Traveling	☐	
	Other	☐	

Barometer

Moon Phase

1st Quarter ☐   ½ Moon ☐   3rd Quarter ☐   Full Moon ☐

Hunt Details

Time	Species	Size	Location	Weapon	Seen	Shot	Lost	Captured

ADDITIONAL COMMENTS

HUNTING LOG

| Date | | Start Time | | End Time | |

| Location | | Longitude | | Latitude | |

| Terrain | |

| Co-Hunter(s) | |

Weather	Activity / Sightings		Gear / Set Up
(Rain, Hot Windy etc.)	Feeding	☐	
	Fresh Droppings	☐	
Temperature	Tracks	☐	
Low High	Traveling	☐	
	Other	☐	

Barometer	Moon Phase
	1st Quarter ☐ ½ Moon ☐ 3rd Quarter ☐ Full Moon ☐

Hunt Details

Time	Species	Size	Location	Weapon	Seen	Shot	Lost	Captured

ADDITIONAL COMMENTS

_____

_____

_____

_____

_____

HUNTING LOG

Date		Start Time		End Time	

Location		Longitude		Latitude	

Terrain

Co-Hunter(s)

Weather	Activity / Sightings		Gear / Set Up
(Rain, Hot Windy etc.)	Feeding	☐	
	Fresh Droppings	☐	
Temperature	Tracks	☐	
Low | High	Traveling	☐	
	Other	☐	

Barometer

Moon Phase

1st Quarter ☐ ½ Moon ☐ 3rd Quarter ☐ Full Moon ☐

Hunt Details

Time	Species	Size	Location	Weapon	Seen	Shot	Lost	Captured

ADDITIONAL COMMENTS

HUNTING LOG

Date		Start Time		End Time	

Location		Longitude		Latitude	

Terrain

Co-Hunter(s)

Weather	Activity / Sightings		Gear / Set Up
(Rain, Hot Windy etc.)	Feeding	☐	
	Fresh Droppings	☐	
Temperature	Tracks	☐	
Low High	Traveling	☐	
	Other	☐	

Barometer   **Moon Phase**

1st Quarter ☐   ½ Moon ☐   3rd Quarter ☐   Full Moon ☐

Hunt Details

Time	Species	Size	Location	Weapon	Seen	Shot	Lost	Captured

ADDITIONAL COMMENTS

_____
_____
_____
_____
_____

HUNTING LOG

Date		Start Time		End Time	

Location | **Longitude** | **Latitude**

Terrain

Co-Hunter(s)

Weather	Activity / Sightings		Gear / Set Up
(Rain, Hot Windy etc.)	Feeding	☐	
	Fresh Droppings	☐	
Temperature	Tracks	☐	
Low | High	Traveling	☐	
	Other	☐	
Barometer	**Moon Phase**		
	1st Quarter ☐ ½ Moon ☐ 3rd Quarter ☐ Full Moon ☐		

Hunt Details

Time	Species	Size	Location	Weapon	Seen	Shot	Lost	Captured

ADDITIONAL COMMENTS

_____
_____
_____
_____
_____

HUNTING LOG

Date

Start Time

End Time

Location

Longitude

Latitude

Terrain

Co-Hunter(s)

Weather	**Activity / Sightings**		**Gear / Set Up**
(Rain, Hot Windy etc.)	Feeding	☐	
	Fresh Droppings	☐	
Temperature	Tracks	☐	
Low | High	Traveling	☐	
	Other	☐	

Barometer

Moon Phase

1st Quarter ☐   ½ Moon ☐   3rd Quarter ☐   Full Moon ☐

Hunt Details

Time	Species	Size	Location	Weapon	Seen	Shot	Lost	Captured

ADDITIONAL COMMENTS

HUNTING LOG

Date		Start Time		End Time	

Location		Longitude		Latitude	

Terrain

Co-Hunter(s)

Weather	Activity / Sightings		Gear / Set Up
(Rain, Hot Windy etc.)	Feeding	☐	
	Fresh Droppings	☐	
Temperature	Tracks	☐	
Low | High	Traveling	☐	
	Other	☐	
Barometer	**Moon Phase**		

1st Quarter ☐   ½ Moon ☐   3rd Quarter ☐   Full Moon ☐

Hunt Details

Time	Species	Size	Location	Weapon	Seen	Shot	Lost	Captured

ADDITIONAL COMMENTS

_____

_____

_____

_____

_____

HUNTING LOG

Date   **Start Time**   **End Time**

Location   **Longitude**   **Latitude**

Terrain

Co-Hunter(s)

Weather (Rain, Hot Windy etc.)	**Activity / Sightings**		**Gear / Set Up**
	Feeding	☐	
	Fresh Droppings	☐	
Temperature	Tracks	☐	
Low High	Traveling	☐	
	Other	☐	
Barometer	**Moon Phase**		
	1st Quarter ☐ ½ Moon ☐ 3rd Quarter ☐ Full Moon ☐		

Hunt Details

Time	Species	Size	Location	Weapon	Seen	Shot	Lost	Captured

ADDITIONAL COMMENTS

_____

_____

_____

_____

_____

HUNTING LOG

Date	Start Time	End Time

Location	Longitude	Latitude

Terrain

Co-Hunter(s)

Weather (Rain, Hot Windy etc.)	**Activity / Sightings**		**Gear / Set Up**
	Feeding	☐	
	Fresh Droppings	☐	
Temperature	Tracks	☐	
Low | High	Traveling	☐	
	Other	☐	
Barometer	**Moon Phase**		
	1st Quarter ☐ ½ Moon ☐ 3rd Quarter ☐ Full Moon ☐		

Hunt Details

Time	Species	Size	Location	Weapon	Seen	Shot	Lost	Captured

ADDITIONAL COMMENTS

HUNTING LOG

Date		Start Time		End Time	

Location		Longitude		Latitude	

Terrain	

Co-Hunter(s)	

Weather	Activity / Sightings		Gear / Set Up
(Rain, Hot Windy etc.)	Feeding	☐	
	Fresh Droppings	☐	
Temperature	Tracks	☐	
Low High	Traveling	☐	
	Other	☐	
Barometer	**Moon Phase**		
	1st Quarter ☐ ½ Moon ☐ 3rd Quarter ☐ Full Moon ☐		

Hunt Details

Time	Species	Size	Location	Weapon	Seen	Shot	Lost	Captured

ADDITIONAL COMMENTS

_____

_____

_____

_____

_____

HUNTING LOG

Date		Start Time		End Time	

Location		Longitude		Latitude	

Terrain	

Co-Hunter(s)	

Weather (Rain, Hot Windy etc.)	Activity / Sightings		Gear / Set Up
	Feeding	☐	
	Fresh Droppings	☐	
Temperature	Tracks	☐	
Low / High	Traveling	☐	
	Other	☐	
Barometer	**Moon Phase**		
	1st Quarter ☐ ½ Moon ☐ 3rd Quarter ☐ Full Moon ☐		

Hunt Details

Time	Species	Size	Location	Weapon	Seen	Shot	Lost	Captured

ADDITIONAL COMMENTS

HUNTING LOG

Date		Start Time		End Time	

Location		Longitude		Latitude	

Terrain

Co-Hunter(s)

Weather (Rain, Hot Windy etc.)	**Activity / Sightings**		**Gear / Set Up**
	Feeding	☐	
	Fresh Droppings	☐	
Temperature	Tracks	☐	
Low / High	Traveling	☐	
	Other	☐	

Barometer — **Moon Phase**

1st Quarter ☐ ½ Moon ☐ 3rd Quarter ☐ Full Moon ☐

Hunt Details

Time	Species	Size	Location	Weapon	Seen	Shot	Lost	Captured

ADDITIONAL COMMENTS

HUNTING LOG

Date	Start Time	End Time

Location	Longitude	Latitude

Terrain

Co-Hunter(s)

Weather	Activity / Sightings	Gear / Set Up
(Rain, Hot Windy etc.)	Feeding ☐	
	Fresh Droppings ☐	
Temperature	Tracks ☐	
Low / High	Traveling ☐	
	Other ☐	

Barometer	Moon Phase
	1st Quarter ☐ ½ Moon ☐ 3rd Quarter ☐ Full Moon ☐

Hunt Details

Time	Species	Size	Location	Weapon	Seen	Shot	Lost	Captured

ADDITIONAL COMMENTS

_____
_____
_____
_____
_____

HUNTING LOG

Date **Start Time** **End Time**

Location **Longitude** **Latitude**

Terrain

Co-Hunter(s)

Weather (Rain, Hot Windy etc.)	**Activity / Sightings**		**Gear / Set Up**
	Feeding	☐	
	Fresh Droppings	☐	
Temperature	Tracks	☐	
Low High	Traveling	☐	
	Other	☐	

Barometer	**Moon Phase**
	1st Quarter ☐ ½ Moon ☐ 3rd Quarter ☐ Full Moon ☐

Hunt Details

Time	Species	Size	Location	Weapon	Seen	Shot	Lost	Captured

ADDITIONAL COMMENTS

_____

_____

_____

_____

_____

HUNTING LOG

Date		Start Time		End Time	

Location		Longitude		Latitude	

Terrain

Co-Hunter(s)

Weather	Activity / Sightings		Gear / Set Up
(Rain, Hot Windy etc.)	Feeding	☐	
	Fresh Droppings	☐	
Temperature	Tracks	☐	
Low · High	Traveling	☐	
	Other	☐	
Barometer	**Moon Phase**		
	1st Quarter ☐ ½ Moon ☐ 3rd Quarter ☐ Full Moon ☐		

Hunt Details

Time	Species	Size	Location	Weapon	Seen	Shot	Lost	Captured

ADDITIONAL COMMENTS

_____

_____

_____

_____

_____

HUNTING LOG

Date		Start Time		End Time	

Location		Longitude		Latitude	

Terrain

Co-Hunter(s)

Weather (Rain, Hot Windy etc.)	Activity / Sightings		Gear / Set Up
	Feeding	☐	
	Fresh Droppings	☐	
Temperature	Tracks	☐	
Low | High	Traveling	☐	
	Other	☐	
Barometer	**Moon Phase**		
	1st Quarter ☐ ½ Moon ☐ 3rd Quarter ☐ Full Moon ☐		

Hunt Details

Time	Species	Size	Location	Weapon	Seen	Shot	Lost	Captured

ADDITIONAL COMMENTS

_____

_____

_____

_____

_____

HUNTING LOG

Date		Start Time		End Time	

Location		Longitude		Latitude	

Terrain	

Co-Hunter(s)	

Weather	Activity / Sightings		Gear / Set Up
(Rain, Hot Windy etc.)	Feeding	☐	
	Fresh Droppings	☐	
Temperature	Tracks	☐	
Low — High	Traveling	☐	
	Other	☐	
Barometer	**Moon Phase**		
	1st Quarter ☐ ½ Moon ☐ 3rd Quarter ☐ Full Moon ☐		

Hunt Details

Time	Species	Size	Location	Weapon	Seen	Shot	Lost	Captured

ADDITIONAL COMMENTS

HUNTING LOG

Date		Start Time		End Time	

Location		Longitude		Latitude	

Terrain

Co-Hunter(s)

Weather (Rain, Hot Windy etc.)	Activity / Sightings	Gear / Set Up

Weather (Rain, Hot Windy etc.)

Activity / Sightings	
Feeding	☐
Fresh Droppings	☐
Tracks	☐
Traveling	☐
Other	☐

Gear / Set Up

Temperature

Low	High

Barometer

Moon Phase

1st Quarter ☐   ½ Moon ☐   3rd Quarter ☐   Full Moon ☐

Hunt Details

Time	Species	Size	Location	Weapon	Seen	Shot	Lost	Captured

ADDITIONAL COMMENTS

_____
_____
_____
_____
_____

HUNTING LOG

Date		Start Time		End Time	

Location		Longitude		Latitude	

Terrain

Co-Hunter(s)

Weather	Activity / Sightings		Gear / Set Up
(Rain, Hot Windy etc.)	Feeding	☐	
	Fresh Droppings	☐	
Temperature	Tracks	☐	
Low | High	Traveling	☐	
	Other	☐	
Barometer	**Moon Phase**		

1st Quarter ☐   ½ Moon ☐   3rd Quarter ☐   Full Moon ☐

Hunt Details

Time	Species	Size	Location	Weapon	Seen	Shot	Lost	Captured

ADDITIONAL COMMENTS

_____
_____
_____
_____
_____

HUNTING LOG

Date		Start Time		End Time	

Location		Longitude		Latitude	

Terrain

Co-Hunter(s)

Weather (Rain, Hot Windy etc.)	**Activity / Sightings**		**Gear / Set Up**
	Feeding	☐	
	Fresh Droppings	☐	
Temperature	Tracks	☐	
Low | High	Traveling	☐	
	Other	☐	
Barometer	**Moon Phase**		
	1st Quarter ☐ ½ Moon ☐ 3rd Quarter ☐ Full Moon ☐		

Hunt Details

Time	Species	Size	Location	Weapon	Seen	Shot	Lost	Captured

ADDITIONAL COMMENTS

HUNTING LOG

85

Date		Start Time		End Time	

Location		Longitude		Latitude	

Terrain	

Co-Hunter(s)	

Weather	Activity / Sightings		Gear / Set Up
(Rain, Hot Windy etc.)	Feeding	☐	
	Fresh Droppings	☐	
Temperature	Tracks	☐	
Low / High	Traveling	☐	
	Other	☐	
Barometer	**Moon Phase**		

1st Quarter ☐   ½ Moon ☐   3rd Quarter ☐   Full Moon ☐

Hunt Details

Time	Species	Size	Location	Weapon	Seen	Shot	Lost	Captured

ADDITIONAL COMMENTS

HUNTING LOG

Date		Start Time		End Time	

Location		Longitude		Latitude	

Terrain

Co-Hunter(s)

Weather (Rain, Hot Windy etc.)	Activity / Sightings		Gear / Set Up
	Feeding ☐		
	Fresh Droppings ☐		
Temperature	Tracks ☐		
Low — High	Traveling ☐		
	Other ☐		
Barometer	**Moon Phase**		
	1st Quarter ☐ ½ Moon ☐ 3rd Quarter ☐ Full Moon ☐		

Hunt Details

Time	Species	Size	Location	Weapon	Seen	Shot	Lost	Captured

ADDITIONAL COMMENTS

_____
_____
_____
_____
_____

HUNTING LOG

Date	Start Time	End Time

Location	Longitude	Latitude

Terrain

Co-Hunter(s)

Weather	Activity / Sightings	Gear / Set Up
(Rain, Hot Windy etc.)	Feeding ☐	
	Fresh Droppings ☐	
Temperature	Tracks ☐	
Low	High	Traveling ☐	
	Other ☐	
Barometer	**Moon Phase**	
	1st Quarter ☐ ½ Moon ☐ 3rd Quarter ☐ Full Moon ☐	

Hunt Details

Time	Species	Size	Location	Weapon	Seen	Shot	Lost	Captured

ADDITIONAL COMMENTS

HUNTING LOG

88

Date		Start Time		End Time	

Location		Longitude		Latitude	

Terrain

Co-Hunter(s)

Weather (Rain, Hot Windy etc.)	**Activity / Sightings**		**Gear / Set Up**
	Feeding	☐	
	Fresh Droppings	☐	
Temperature	Tracks	☐	
Low High	Traveling	☐	
	Other	☐	
Barometer	**Moon Phase**		
	1st Quarter ☐ ½ Moon ☐ 3rd Quarter ☐ Full Moon ☐		

Hunt Details

Time	Species	Size	Location	Weapon	Seen	Shot	Lost	Captured

ADDITIONAL COMMENTS

_____

_____

_____

_____

_____

HUNTING LOG

| Date | | Start Time | | End Time | |

| Location | | Longitude | | Latitude | |

| Terrain | |

| Co-Hunter(s) | |

Weather
(Rain, Hot Windy etc.)

Temperature

| Low | High |

Barometer

Activity / Sightings

Feeding	☐
Fresh Droppings	☐
Tracks	☐
Traveling	☐
Other	☐

Gear / Set Up

Moon Phase

1st Quarter ☐ ½ Moon ☐ 3rd Quarter ☐ Full Moon ☐

Hunt Details

Time	Species	Size	Location	Weapon	Seen	Shot	Lost	Captured

ADDITIONAL COMMENTS

HUNTING LOG

Date	Start Time	End Time

Location	Longitude	Latitude

Terrain

Co-Hunter(s)

Weather (Rain, Hot Windy etc.)	**Activity / Sightings**		**Gear / Set Up**
	Feeding	☐	
	Fresh Droppings	☐	
Temperature	Tracks	☐	
Low High	Traveling	☐	
	Other	☐	
Barometer	**Moon Phase**		
	1st Quarter ☐ ½ Moon ☐ 3rd Quarter ☐ Full Moon ☐		

Hunt Details

Time	Species	Size	Location	Weapon	Seen	Shot	Lost	Captured

ADDITIONAL COMMENTS

_____
_____
_____
_____
_____

HUNTING LOG

Date		Start Time		End Time	

Location		Longitude		Latitude	

Terrain

Co-Hunter(s)

Weather	Activity / Sightings		Gear / Set Up
(Rain, Hot Windy etc.)	Feeding	☐	
	Fresh Droppings	☐	
Temperature	Tracks	☐	
Low High	Traveling	☐	
	Other	☐	

Barometer   **Moon Phase**

1st Quarter ☐   ½ Moon ☐   3rd Quarter ☐   Full Moon ☐

Hunt Details

Time	Species	Size	Location	Weapon	Seen	Shot	Lost	Captured

ADDITIONAL COMMENTS

HUNTING LOG

Date		Start Time		End Time	
Location		Longitude		Latitude	
Terrain					
Co-Hunter(s)					

Weather	Activity / Sightings		Gear / Set Up
(Rain, Hot Windy etc.)	Feeding ☐		
	Fresh Droppings ☐		
Temperature	Tracks ☐		
Low | High	Traveling ☐		
	Other ☐		
Barometer	**Moon Phase**		
	1st Quarter ☐ ½ Moon ☐ 3rd Quarter ☐ Full Moon ☐		

Hunt Details

Time	Species	Size	Location	Weapon	Seen	Shot	Lost	Captured

ADDITIONAL COMMENTS

HUNTING LOG

Date		Start Time		End Time	

Location		Longitude		Latitude	

Terrain

Co-Hunter(s)

Weather	Activity / Sightings		Gear / Set Up
(Rain, Hot Windy etc.)	Feeding	☐	
	Fresh Droppings	☐	
Temperature	Tracks	☐	
Low High	Traveling	☐	
	Other	☐	
Barometer	**Moon Phase**		
	1st Quarter ☐ ½ Moon ☐ 3rd Quarter ☐ Full Moon ☐		

Hunt Details

Time	Species	Size	Location	Weapon	Seen	Shot	Lost	Captured

ADDITIONAL COMMENTS

HUNTING LOG

Date   **Start Time**   **End Time**

Location   **Longitude**   **Latitude**

Terrain

Co-Hunter(s)

Weather (Rain, Hot Windy etc.)	Activity / Sightings		Gear / Set Up
	Feeding	☐	
	Fresh Droppings	☐	
Temperature	Tracks	☐	
Low High	Traveling	☐	
	Other	☐	

Barometer	**Moon Phase**
	1st Quarter ☐ ½ Moon ☐ 3rd Quarter ☐ Full Moon ☐

Hunt Details

Time	Species	Size	Location	Weapon	Seen	Shot	Lost	Captured

ADDITIONAL COMMENTS

_____

_____

_____

_____

_____

HUNTING LOG

Date		Start Time		End Time	

Location		Longitude		Latitude	

Terrain

Co-Hunter(s)

Weather	Activity / Sightings		Gear / Set Up
(Rain, Hot Windy etc.)	Feeding	☐	
	Fresh Droppings	☐	
Temperature	Tracks	☐	
Low | High	Traveling	☐	
	Other	☐	
Barometer	**Moon Phase**		

1st Quarter ☐   ½ Moon ☐   3rd Quarter ☐   Full Moon ☐

Hunt Details

Time	Species	Size	Location	Weapon	Seen	Shot	Lost	Captured

ADDITIONAL COMMENTS

_____

_____

_____

_____

_____

HUNTING LOG

Date		Start Time		End Time	

Location		Longitude		Latitude	

Terrain	

Co-Hunter(s)	

Weather
(Rain, Hot Windy etc.)

Temperature
Low	High

Barometer

Activity / Sightings

Feeding	☐
Fresh Droppings	☐
Tracks	☐
Traveling	☐
Other	☐

Gear / Set Up

Moon Phase

1st Quarter ☐ ½ Moon ☐ 3rd Quarter ☐ Full Moon ☐

Hunt Details

Time	Species	Size	Location	Weapon	Seen	Shot	Lost	Captured

ADDITIONAL COMMENTS

HUNTING LOG

Date		Start Time		End Time	

Location | **Longitude** | **Latitude**

Terrain

Co-Hunter(s)

Weather	Activity / Sightings		Gear / Set Up
(Rain, Hot Windy etc.)	Feeding	☐	
	Fresh Droppings	☐	
Temperature	Tracks	☐	
Low High	Traveling	☐	
	Other	☐	

Barometer	**Moon Phase**
	1st Quarter ☐ ½ Moon ☐ 3rd Quarter ☐ Full Moon ☐

Hunt Details

Time	Species	Size	Location	Weapon	Seen	Shot	Lost	Captured

ADDITIONAL COMMENTS

_____

_____

_____

_____

_____

HUNTING LOG

Date **Start Time** **End Time**

Location **Longitude** **Latitude**

Terrain

Co-Hunter(s)

Weather (Rain, Hot Windy etc.)	Activity / Sightings		Gear / Set Up
	Feeding	☐	
	Fresh Droppings	☐	
Temperature	Tracks	☐	
Low　　High	Traveling	☐	
	Other	☐	

Barometer	**Moon Phase**
	1st Quarter ☐　½ Moon ☐　3rd Quarter ☐　Full Moon ☐

Hunt Details

Time	Species	Size	Location	Weapon	Seen	Shot	Lost	Captured

ADDITIONAL COMMENTS

_____

_____

_____

_____

_____

HUNTING LOG

Date	Start Time	End Time

Location	Longitude	Latitude

Terrain

Co-Hunter(s)

Weather	Activity / Sightings	Gear / Set Up
(Rain, Hot Windy etc.)	Feeding ☐	
	Fresh Droppings ☐	
Temperature	Tracks ☐	
Low High	Traveling ☐	
	Other ☐	
Barometer	**Moon Phase**	
	1st Quarter ☐ ½ Moon ☐ 3rd Quarter ☐ Full Moon ☐	

Hunt Details

Time	Species	Size	Location	Weapon	Seen	Shot	Lost	Captured

ADDITIONAL COMMENTS

_____

_____

_____

_____

_____

HUNTING LOG

Date		Start Time		End Time	

Location		Longitude		Latitude	

Terrain

Co-Hunter(s)

Weather (Rain, Hot Windy etc.)	**Activity / Sightings**		**Gear / Set Up**
	Feeding	☐	
	Fresh Droppings	☐	
Temperature	Tracks	☐	
Low / High	Traveling	☐	
	Other	☐	
Barometer	**Moon Phase**		
	1st Quarter ☐ ½ Moon ☐ 3rd Quarter ☐ Full Moon ☐		

Hunt Details

Time	Species	Size	Location	Weapon	Seen	Shot	Lost	Captured

ADDITIONAL COMMENTS

Made in the USA
Monee, IL
09 February 2021

59901107R00059